AN ENTREPRENEUR'S
TRAIL
GUIDE

For Entrepreneurs and their Coaches

ANDREA SIGETICH

Dedication

To the 300+ students of professional coaching who have put up with my singing, my occasional humor, my dancing, my often getting lost in my own words. You are the inspiration behind this book. Much more important, you are an inspiration and bright shining light in the world. You know who you are. I love each and every one of you.

Acknowledgements

My illustrator, Jerry Scheller, brought my ideas to life! Thank you for your energy, flexibility, and creativity, Jerry.

A few extraordinary coaches in Bend Oregon, over Pinot Gris and Tuna Poke, inspired me to keep my boots on the trail. Thank you to my friends Leslie Koc, Sheila Mawdsley, and Jillian Taylor.

And finally, I wish to express deep gratitude to my extraordinarily bright and insightful readers: Donna Billings, Dennis Doherty, Carole Katz, and once again and forever, my rock and my own personal trail guide, Beryl Rullman.

For Entrepreneurs and their Coaches

I hear you are embarking on a great adventure! You're starting your own business, perhaps as a mediator or an attorney or a professional coach. Or maybe you are self-publishing books or designing websites. Exciting, isn't it? And a bit daunting, too. If you want to Do more of what you want to do, and Be more of who you want to be, you've come to the right place. Welcome!

One thing you know for certain, whether your adventure is brand new or you've been at it for a few months or years ... you know that you don't want to live by someone else's rules. You know your path is unique. You can't follow someone else's trail; it just isn't going to happen that way.

An Entrepreneur's Trail Guide is a workbook conceived and designed by a fellow entrepreneur, so you can explore and design your own unique trail. The steps in *An Entrepreneur's Trail Guide* are presented in logical order. However, if you have a great idea about a milestone, which doesn't come until halfway through, flip to the milestone page and capture it. You can't do it wrong. It is, after all, your trail!

Whether you are working in the trail guide on your own, or with the support of a professional coach or a group of like-minded friends, you decide your pace. However, I suggest you work through the trail guide in small bite-sized pieces. Take a page, write or draw your thoughts, and then let it stew for a while. Take it to your coach. No need to hurry it along. Remember, as with any journey, whether a car trip, a train ride or a hiking path in the wilderness, the travel IS the journey.

What makes *An Entrepreneur's Trail Guide* unique is we will explore your inner self – your strengths, values, life purpose, genius, inner wise captain and sometimes-present saboteurs – as well what you do in the world. You will find resources, including blank forms you can print from *An Entrepreneur's Trail Guide* at the website SageCoach.com/SageEntrepreneur. Go visit and download all you need!

Why "Sage Entrepreneur?" A Sage is a profoundly wise person. That's you! Our work will illuminate your own sagacity, inciting your inner wisdom so that you make the most effective choices in your entrepreneurial adventure. The Sage is also a plant with healing qualities, and is prolific in the desert and in my back yard. The deserts of the western United States in all their magnificence, agony, impact, and awesome quiet, are the inspiration behind the work of SageCoach and SageEntrepreneur.

Our mission is to bring out the Sage in YOU! Welcome to your own adventure!

CONTENTS

EXPLORE THE TERRAIN

Explore the Terrain – In this first step of *An Entrepreneur's Trail Guide*, we delve deeply into who you are today. We do this so that you have a foundation from which to start dreaming. We also do this to acknowledge all you have been and the journey you have taken to bring you to the person you are today. Page 5.

IMAGINE THE TRAIL'S END

In Imagine the Trail's End you suspend current reality and dream deeply. What do you truly desire? Who do you want to be? What do you want to do? Page 19.

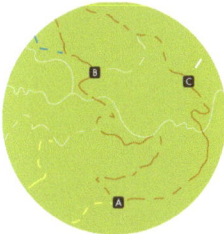

MAP YOUR TRAIL

As you come to clearly recognize the gaps between your present state and your imagined future, you'll ask yourself … what are the strategies that compel me to reach my imagined future? Page 37.

BOOTS ON!

In this step, you implement your strategies. Step by step, with your boots supporting and protecting your feet, you travel towards your destination. Page 55.

RELISH THE VIEW

Now you have arrived at the top. Here is where you Be all you choose to be, and Do all you choose to do. Page 69.

ARE YOU READY? WHAT ARE YOU MOST EXCITED ABOUT?

◎ Write your thoughts here!

EXPLORE
the TERRAIN

WHAT'S IN YOUR PACK?

Throughout *An Entrepreneur's Trail Guide* are text boxes titled "What's in Your Pack?" These pages describe the essential tools you already have in your pack. You may use these items at any time in your entrepreneurial adventure.

IN YOUR HIKING PACK …

1.   Navigation (map and compass)
2.   Sun protection (sunglasses and sunscreen)
3.   Insulation (extra clothing for rain and warmth)
4.   Illumination (headlamp/flashlight)
5.   First-aid kit
6.   Fire (waterproof matches/lighter/candles)
7.   Nutrition (extra food)
8.   Hydration (water and a way to purify trail water)
9.   Noise (a whistle is best)
10. Knife (or multi-purpose tool)

IN YOUR ENTREPRENEURIAL PACK …

1.   Coach
2.   Your Genius
3.   Choice
4.   BOSI (a quiz about your entrepreneurial style)
5.   Captain & Saboteur Management
6.   Exercise
7.   Affirmations
8.   Support Team
9.   Mindfulness
10. Celebration

EXPLORE THE TERRAIN

We begin at a great place, by exploring the terrain where you are right now. After all, you can't make it to your destination if you don't know where you are starting from. Do you travel north or south, or south/southeast? What is the terrain right here at the beginning? Are you in the Cascade Mountains, the Sonoran desert, or a thickly wooded hillside in Pennsylvania? Let's find out who you are as you embark on the adventurer's journey. Let's explore all you are bringing to the beginning of the journey, the tools in your pack, the strengths you offer, the purpose of your intention.

In this step, we delve deeply into who you are today. We do this so that you have a solid foundation from which to start dreaming. We also do this to acknowledge all you have been and the journey you have taken to bring you to the whole person you are today. Even though this step has a sense of impatience attached to it – the desire to move on to the vision is palpable – this self-discovery is grounding and serves to honor and acknowledge who you are right now. So grab your pens or your colored pencils and begin.

WHAT'S IN YOUR PACK #1 – A COACH

Hiring a Professional Coach is the single action that trumps all the others in *An Entrepreneur's Trail Guide*. A certified, well-trained, and experienced entrepreneur coach will guide you through the journey in this book, and will ensure that you have all that is essential to your success. That's where *An Entrepreneur's Trail Guide* came from ... the experiences of entrepreneurs working with a professional coach.

If you utilize the Trail Guide AND work with an entrepreneur coach, you'll multiply the positive effect on you and your entrepreneurial business. So, what's stopping you? Get started now!

CHOOSING A COACH

What do you imagine to be your ideal relationship with a professional coach?
What qualities are essential in your coach?
How will you find the perfect coach for you?

"He who knows others is wise. He who knows himself is enlightened."
–LOA-TZU

MY STRENGTHS

How can you recognize your natural, innate talents and unearth your magnificent strengths? *StrengthsFinder 2.0* is a useful assessment for identifying strengths. To complete this assessment, purchase a book that supplies you with a code for taking the instrument one time. We recommend *StrengthsFinder 2.0* by Tom Rath (Gallup Press, 2007). Discovering your strengths helps you to focus your energy and to choose actions that are likely to lead to success. Know and leverage your strengths to achieve what you want to achieve, with ease.

STEP ONE: List all Possible Strengths

After you have completed *StrengthsFinder 2.0* and received the report of your top five strengths, add strengths you believe are missing. Remember that strengths are not your experiences, but rather, your talents and gifts. Also list your passions. Some useful questions to ask yourself:

- *At what do I excel?*
- *What is easy for me?*
- *What do I enjoy?*
- *What are my passions?*

STEP TWO: Uncover Themes

Group your strengths into "buckets" or categories that represent your deepest and most powerful strengths. Assign a working "theme" to each bucket. For example, you might combine your strengths of ideation (from *StrengthsFinder 2.0*) your curiosity, and your creativity into a strength bucket you call "innovation."

STEP THREE: Name the Game You'll Play

Even if you are not 100% certain you've created the perfect list of your strengths, go ahead and name them. Try to create no more than five named strengths so you can remember them and work with them. Naming your strengths is an important step. Assigning a name to a strength makes that strength more tangible and real and easier to access than a strength that is loose, unclear, and amorphous. For example, I named my strengths of innovation and ideation and creativity one word – creativity.

STEP FOUR: Observe Yourself

Over a two week period, notice where you excel. Notice, too, when you become engaged, enthused, excited, inspired, intrigued, or passionate! These purely emotional reactions are important because they offer clues to your deepest strengths.

Ask yourself these questions:
- *Which of these strengths give me deep joy?*
- *Which strengths are fun to use?*
- *What strength am I most inspired to use?*
- *What strength is most interesting and intriguing to me?*

Adjust your named strengths; rename them as needed so they feel right.

MY STRENGTHS

You know who you THINK you are … but truly, how do you show up to others? This is an enlightening and affirming exercise to learn about how you appear to others, and the impact you have. When I did this exercise, I was astonished and delighted to see how often "playful" came up in the responses. So much so, that I began to change my marketing materials, how I coached, how I facilitated. I thought I was ultra-serious and this exercise helped me to affirm the strengths I knew about, and to discover some brand new ones!

Identify 25 or 30 people (really!) who know you well They can be people you work with, friends and family, anyone you have engaged with over time. Then send them an e-mail. Do NOT ask them for your strengths! You'll receive standard responses about experience and skills if you ask for "strengths." The last seven words of this e-mail are what make this exercise work well.

"I am doing some work to identify my personal brand. I would appreciate your input! Please take a minute and, by return e-mail, tell me the three or four words that you believe describe the essence of me."

"It is with the soul that we grasp the essence of another human being, not with the mind, nor even with the heart."
—HENRY MILLER

- Write your Essence words here.
- Circle words that are the same or similar.
- Notice the patterns that emerge.
- What surprises you?
- What excites you and lights you up?
- Add to your strengths list any word that speaks to you.

WHAT'S IN YOUR PACK #2 – YOUR GENIUS

We each have a genius ... a special and unique talent for making a difference in the world. Those who uncover their "Genius" are able to create a clear direction, purpose, strategy and action. Those who are unclear can make false starts and actions that undermine us. A simple way to articulate your Genius is a two word statement, with an "ing" verb and a noun. Here are some examples:

- Digging Deeper
- Finding the Positive
- Generating Warmth
- Inciting Perspectives (this is mine!)

I have worked with a number of people who do "Genius" work – and there is a simple resource I want to point you to. Purchase a copy of *Is Your Genius at Work?* by Dick Richards. Read the book, do the exercises. Your Genius will prove an excellent foundation moving forward with your business.

MY GENIUS IS ...

_____

BALANCE STAR

Work/life balance is very important to an entrepreneur. As a matter of fact, studies show the lack of life balance is a major cause of entrepreneurial failure. Right from the start, you want to think of your whole life as you design your business venture, so that you are taking care of yourself physically, mentally, emotionally, socially, and spiritually. When you do this, you can be the BEST entrepreneur.

A tool you can use is the "Balance Star." Complete your own Balance Star, using a 1 to 10 scale; identify your level of satisfaction. One means, "I am very dissatisfied with this space in my life." Ten means, "This space is great!"

Note this is not a request to draw the amount of resources you are committing to each segment, but your current satisfaction. You may, for example, spend only 30 minutes each week on spiritual pursuits. However, that may be precisely what you wish to spend, and your satisfaction level might be a 9 or a 10. The model below demonstrates what a completed Balance Star may look like.

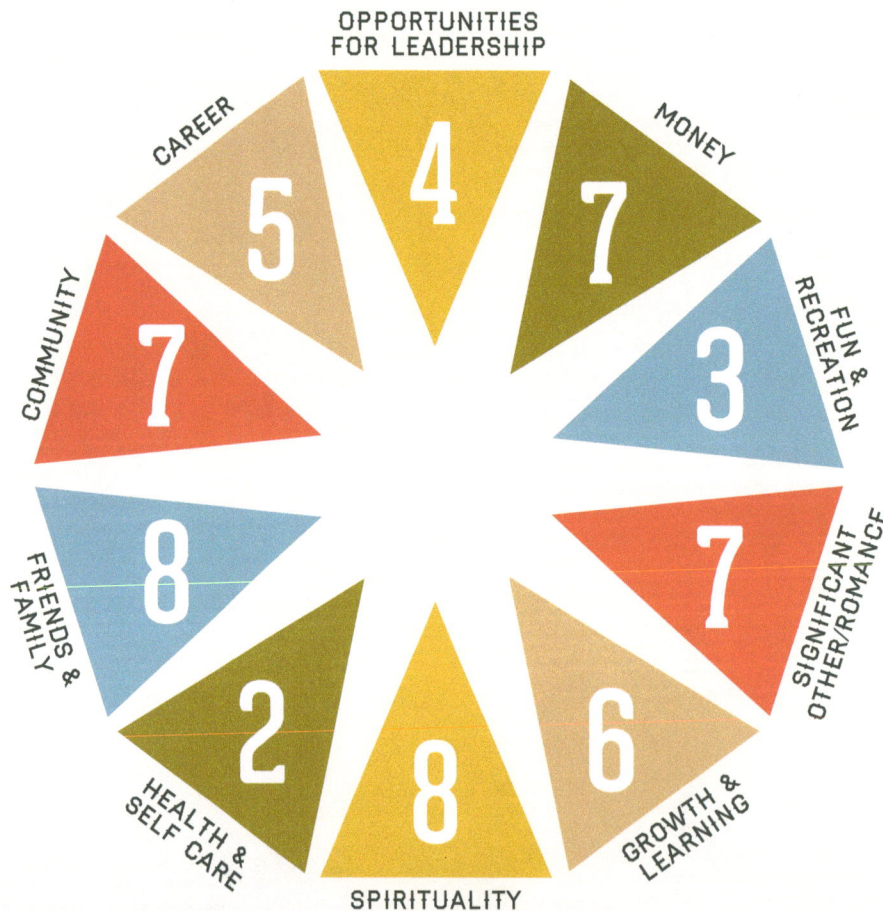

Balance Star segments:
- OPPORTUNITIES FOR LEADERSHIP — 4
- MONEY — 7
- FUN & RECREATION — 3
- SIGNIFICANT OTHER/ROMANCE — 7
- GROWTH & LEARNING — 6
- SPIRITUALITY — 8
- HEALTH & SELF CARE — 2
- FRIENDS & FAMILY — 8
- COMMUNITY — 7
- CAREER — 5

What actions do I want to take to raise my levels of satisfaction?

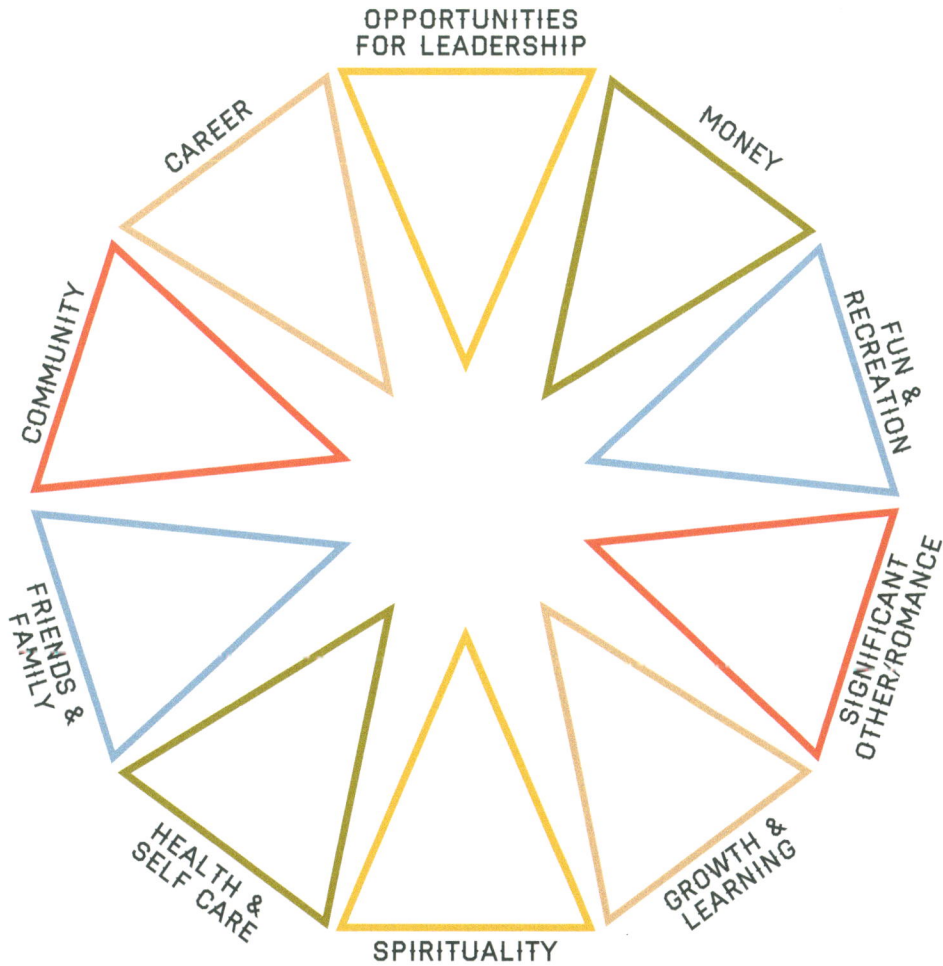

OPPORTUNITIES FOR LEADERSHIP

CAREER

MONEY

COMMUNITY

FUN & RECREATION

SIGNIFICANT OTHER/ROMANCE

FRIENDS & FAMILY

GROWTH & LEARNING

HEALTH & SELF CARE

SPIRITUALITY

Your values are the signposts, the trail markers of life. Fulfillment, happiness, and satisfaction are achieved only when we are aligned with our core values. Unfortunately, few of us learn to distinguish and articulate our own values. As we grow up, we are taught "values." Our well-intentioned parents or others who raised us, our churches or synagogues, schools, mentors work to instill in us good "values." Actually, however, what they are attempting to instill are cultural norms and morals, even if the dominant "culture" is simply the family in which we live.

Our task as adults is to identify and differentiate between the values that we truly hold dear, and the ones that we feel we "should" hold because our society instilled them in us. Values are yours, and they are unique to you. No two of us hold exactly the same values defined in exactly the same way. Your values MUST be met for you to feel satisfied and fulfilled. You can discover your values by looking especially at what you must have, do, or be

to feel satisfied. You can also find your values by looking at what makes you peaceful and content. The opposite is also often true – you may find your values by considering what angers or upsets you or makes you sad.

Values are typically not tangible things we can see or hold. Many clients, when they first begin to identify their core values, use words like "family" and "money" and "wind-surfing." These are actually manifestations of values. "Family" may be a way in which we manifest a value of intimacy, or love, or personal growth. "Money" may be a way in which we actualize a value of "independence" or "freedom" or "pleasure." "Wind-surfing" may actually be a physical expression of a value of "adventure" or "risk" or "carefree physicality." A good phrase to complete, to help you clarify the underlying value is, "_____is a value I hold" instead of "I value _____."

BRAINSTORMING VALUES

STEP ONE: **Begin by brainstorming some possible values**
Try for 20 or even 30. Here are some you can try on for size ...

1) Authenticity is a value I hold
2) Creativity is a value I hold
3) Spontaneity is a value I hold

Ok ... Your turn. At least twenty of them!

STEP TWO: **Combine similar values to arrive at six or so "strings"**
Like this ...

1) Creativity/imagination/design
2) Solitude/introversion/alone

Create six value strings. If a metaphor pops for you ... that's okay! For example, the value string creativity/imagination/design might morph into a value "Picasso." Great!

STEP THREE: **Rate each value on a scale of 1 to ten**
Ten is, "I live this value every day" and one is, "this value is important to me, but I never seem to get around to doing it or being it."

LIFE PURPOSE

Whoa, now THAT is a big concept! Life purpose? Like, why I am here, on this planet, and what I'm supposed to do while I am here? Heck if I know!

And yet, at some level, you DO know. Truly, deep inside you, you know. Let's see if we can take the mystery out of it. There are two essential qualities to a life purpose. First, it makes maximum use of your strengths ... your unique talents and gifts. Second, your life purpose contributes something of value to the world, usually something to people, though once I met someone whose life purpose was about animals.

Here are some statements that are NOT your life purpose. It is not your life purpose to "live in accordance with god's plan." Sorry. If you hold that to be true in your life, great. But it is a non-answer to the question, "What is my life purpose?" What is the plan god had for you? That is the mystery for you to uncover! And it returns to the giving of your gifts.

The second statement I often hear is "my life purpose is to raise happy and well-adjusted children." Again, that's a non-answer. Raising great kids is simply an avenue for your life purpose to play itself out. Yes, that's right. It is the same with your work. Even if you have found your life's work (and I hope you have - that is why you are working in this trail guide) your perfect and ideal work is simply a pathway for you to live your life purpose.

Here are some questions to get you moving towards your purpose. A great way to state your purpose is in this format ... I am the <noun> who <does this> so that <impact>. Like this: "I am the light that illuminates the path for people to find deep joy." Or "I am the dynamite that blows up people's inner critic."

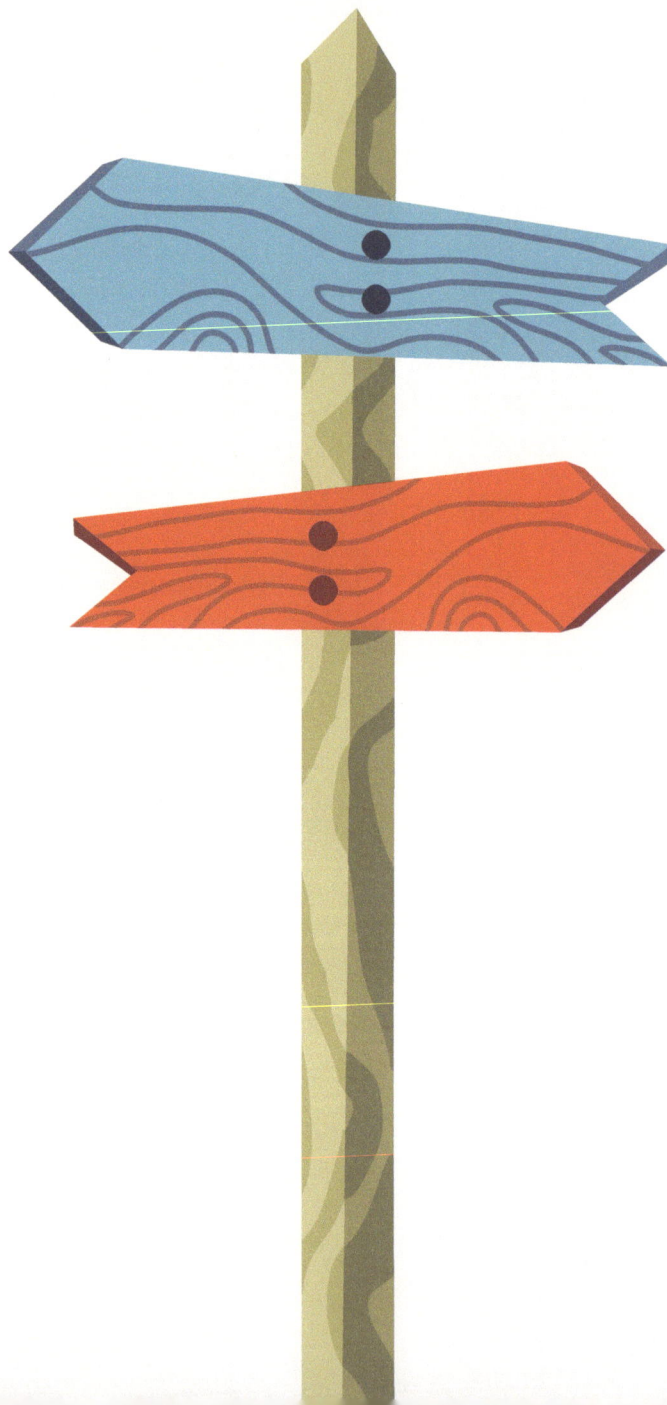

EXPLORING MY LIFE PURPOSE

◉ What strength or gift or talent do you long to give?

◉ What impact do you deeply desire to have in the world? And for whom?

◉ If you could wave a magic wand and make one change in the world, what would it be?

◉ What impact do you have NOW? (Flip back to The Essence of Me" exercise.)

◉ What would not get done if you were not here?

Life is about the gray areas. Things are seldom black and white, even when we wish they were and think they should be, and I like exploring this nuanced terrain.
—EMILY GIFFIN

Choice is an entrepreneur's most potent tool. You always have choice. When you become an entrepreneur, many choices suddenly open up to you. You choose the services you provide, the name of your business, the hours you work, your phone system, your marketing plan, your collaborators and partners. You choose to be happy or fearful, worried or delighted, energetic or defeated. It is all, every bit of it, your choice.

Sometimes all this choice feels overwhelming. Sometimes it feels empowering. Choosing is the way out of discouragement and confusion and apathy. You can always choose optimism, clarity, and passion instead.

It is true that you don't choose all of the situations and circumstances of your life. However, you ALWAYS choose how you respond to those situations and circumstances, even if you are unaware of the choice you are making. If the economy takes a nosedive and your business opportunities fall off, you can choose to bemoan the situation, or you can choose to use the time to pre-write your blog postings. You can always choose who you will be ... your attitudes, perspectives, viewpoints, reactions, actions.

Choice is your most potent tool because it always saves your butt; it pulls you out of the doldrums; it empowers and engages you. Use choice liberally ... it is the spice of the sage entrepreneur.

IMAGINE
the TRAIL'S END

When I hike (which I do as often as the sunshine beckons), there is always a lunch spot ... a beautiful or peaceful spot where I stop, pause, contemplate, and eat! On the Horse Lake trail, it is a gorgeous rocky peninsula that juts far into the serene high Cascade mountain lake, Horse. My destination when climbing up on the Tam MacArthur Trail is an amazing ridge that unfolds a panoramic view of the Cascades.

What is the spectacular scenario/picture/story that you imagine at the end of the trail you are following right now? Vision drives us in every action we take. A mini-vision inspires us even when we plan dinner or embark on a project or walk the dogs.

Where do you want to go?

Take some time away from your office, your kitchen table, or the chair where you do your email. If you attempt to vision in one of these locations, your vision will be small, subdued by the familiarity of the place and the subtle pull towards the status quo. When it is time to vision (and the time is now!) take yourself out of the familiar. Go to a park, or a library or an art museum.

In Imagine the Trail's End we suspend current reality and dream deeply. What do we truly desire? Who do we want to be? What do we want to do? What physical manifestations of living on this earth matter to us? If we are our best self, our future self, how does that person show up in the world? What is compelling for us? What are we drawn towards? What is calling us? Who are we becoming? What do we choose?

All of the components of Explore the Terrain are included in Imagine the Trail's End. The future vision contains all we want to be, all we want to do, and the bridges between these two. Here we work to legitimize the wants, the desires, the compelling way. We DO deserve to create the life we choose. In fact, there is no other life than the one we choose. In Imagine the Trail's End, we choose to articulate and infuse that life with energy. There are many tools available to us here, including vision boards, vision stories, interviewing the future self, imagining in your mind, drawing with colors and photos.

"Would you tell me, please, which way I ought to go from here?"
"That depends a good deal on where you want to get to," said the Cat.
"I don't much care where–" said Alice.
"Then it doesn't matter which way you go," said the Cat.
"–so long as I get SOMEWHERE," Alice added as an explanation.
"Oh, you're sure to do that," said the Cat, "if you only walk long enough."
–LEWIS CARROLL

IMAGINING & VISIONING

There are a myriad ways to imagine (or envision) the Trail's End. No matter which tools you select, there is one rule: do NOT allow current reality to diminish your vision. You will have plenty of time for that later. Right now, you must imagine as clearly as you can the vision you desire to create. And please, for goodness sake, do not only imagine your entrepreneurial vision; imagine your whole life. This is the single biggest mistake made by failed entrepreneurs: they don't consider their whole life when they create their business design and plan. Then, with no allowance for time with the kids, being alone, renewal time, time to eat and sleep and play, they burn out.

I suggest you engage your right brain in this process. It's the intuitive, subjective and creative part of you. Your left brain, logical and analytic, doesn't know what it doesn't know.

First pick a date for your Trail's End. Pick a date as far away as you can possibly imagine. The first time I did this, I picked 20 years. The further out you imagine, the richer and fuller your vision will be, and the clearer the path will be. When you pick a close-in date, say a year or two, you end up with an action plan to accomplish a goal, not a vision. So, even if you can't wrap your head around 20 years, pick ten if possible; five at the lowest end. Picture yourself on your target date.

Write your date here: _____

On the next few pages, you'll find some exercises to help you imagine that day. Do them all, or pick just one. Whatever works for you.

WHAT'S IN YOUR PACK #4 – BOSI

This insightful self-assessment will save you lots of grief when you wonder why your business isn't as successful as Jo's, or you find yourself being jealous when you read about a startup that was just purchased for mega millions. We all start our entrepreneurial adventure for different reasons. Take the BOSI to clarify your reasons, and to assist you in saying yes and no to marketing opportunities, ideas for growing your business, and just plain allocating your time.

http://bosi.in/gHmzJ

Builder?
Opportunist?
Specialist?
Innovator?

WAKING UP ON MY IDEAL DAY

Imagine yourself waking up to your ideal day on the date you have chosen for your vision. Describe in excessive detail what your day is like. Moment by moment, what do you do? Who do you see? How are you engaging your life purpose? What are you doing for yourself physically, emotionally, and spiritually? Who are the clients that appear? If you have wine in the evening, what wine do you have and who do you share it with? Where are you living? Very specifically, what does your house look like? What colors, styles, fabrics? What about your office? Where is it? What does it look like? What furniture and art graces the space? What people do you see in this day and what do you do with them?

WAKING UP ON MY IDEAL DAY

You awaken, refreshed. You stretch, and pop out of bed. The first thing you notice is …

VISION BOARD

A Vision Board is a visual representation of your vision. You'll need a large poster board, a glue stick, scissors, colorful sticky notes, and drawing supplies such as markers or crayons.

There are many ways to create your vision board. There are left brain (logical and analytical) and right brain (intuitive and creative) options. A fun way to create your vision is to gather a pile of magazines. Include some that you receive now and some that are NOT like ones you have around the house today. Make certain they have lots of photos! Then, give yourself a few hours of quiet. Perhaps with a cup of tea by your side, tear out photos and words that resonate with you. Trust your intuition ... don't just do a rational or logical tear. If the blue polka dot shirt grabs your fancy, tear it out and toss it onto your pile! You may ultimately come to understand that it reflects a desire to dress and express yourself more creatively.

When you are complete with the magazine tearing and have a large pile of photos (no fewer than 30 or 40), begin to cut and paste the images that most speak to you on the poster board. Remember to keep yourself grounded and present in the vision date you have chosen – 5 or 10 or 20 years hence. Allow yourself to be immersed in that date, and capture the images that represent who you will be and what you will do in that future time frame.

You may want to supplement your magazine photos with sticky notes, drawings, arrows, exclamation points.

ALTERNATIVE: You can also skip the magazine step if you are very clear about your vision and simply allow it to appear on your poster board by imagining and drawing. Let your inner artist emerge (but remember, your Vision Board is for your eyes only, unless you choose to share it with someone close!)

VISION BOARD

Begin your Vision Board here.
Grab some colored markers and begin to identify bits and pieces that resonate.
Find a time in your calendar to schedule three hours to physically create your Vision Board.
Let you inner child out and have fun! No one will grade your Vision Board!

INTERVIEWING MY FUTURE SELF

Close your eyes, and take a few deep breaths. In and out, in and out. Relax and empty your mind as best as you can. You're going on a short side trail to meet your Future Self. (The entire guided meditation is on the website, SageCoach.com/SageEntrepreneur – this is an abbreviated version.)

Picture a perfect place, a place where you are safe, and where you can be fully yourself. You can make up this place. It might be a cabin in the mountains, a beach house on the ocean, a loft overlooking Pike Place Market. Picture yourself enjoying the space, being cozy and comfortable. Perhaps there is a fire in the fireplace. Perhaps you can hear waves crashing. Perhaps your colorful artwork is on display everywhere you gaze.

In a moment, a very special person will enter your space. You've invited your Future Self for a cup of tea. Your excitement is palpable. Here he comes now – you,

20 years from now. You, dreams fulfilled. You, being all you can be. Let him or her in, and sit down together with your cups of tea.

You may ask your Future Self anything you want. Here are a few questions to get you started:

- Future Self, what do I need to know now to help me become you? (pause and listen to the response)
- Future Self, what wisdom do you want to share with me? (pause and listen)
- Future Self, who do I need to be? (pause and listen)
- Future Self, what name shall I call you by? (pause and listen)

Your Future Self has a gift for you. Reach out and take it. Then ask your Future Self any other questions you wish. When you are complete, thank your Future Self and walk her to the door.

- ⊙ What insights did you gain from your Future Self?

- ⊙ What is the gift you received from your Future Self?

- ⊙ What is your Future Self's name?

- ⊙ Know that you can call up your Future Self any time you like for a conversation. When will you have another conversation?

WHEN MY LIFE IS MOST IDEAL

This is a fun and easy exercise, and it provides important information for creating a rich, resonant, and complete vision. Anything goes! This is a full-on, no-inhibition brainstorm. Ask yourself the simple question, "when is my life most ideal?" You may want to reach back into your life to remember peak moments, or moments you were in the "zone." You may want to look forward to dream. Answer with as many answers as you can. Here are some ideas to get you started.

When is my life most ideal?

- When I'm sitting on a beach
- When I'm feeling physically fit
- When I'm with my spouse
- When I'm turning on light bulbs
- When I'm having a glass of wine with my best friend
- When I'm laughing

28

- What patterns do you notice?
- Which items on this list do you want more of?
- What do you want to do about that?

WHAT'S IN YOUR PACK #5 – THE CAPTAIN & THE SABOTEUR

Within each of us is an inner wise voice. The wise voice is the part of us that knows. It knows what is best for us. It knows our own truth. There are many names for this inner knowing. Some call it the Future Self, some call it Wise One, and I have one client who calls it John. In my work with the Coaches Training Institute, we call it the Captain …"O captain, my captain!" It matters not how you conceive of the Captain. What matters is that you learn to hear the voice of your Captain; that you engage in conversation with your Captain; that you listen. If you have not yet met your captain, there is a guided meditation on our website, SageCoach.com/SageEntrepreneur.

Who is your Captain? What name do you call him or her? (Mine is named "Color Maker").
How do you access your inner wise voice? When do you access it?
What will you do to build your communication with your Captain?

While the Captain can be a little amorphous and hard to meet, I have yet to discover anyone who is not intimately connected with their Saboteur. Some call the Saboteur the Gremlin or the Inner Critic. But it seems everyone knows (oh too well!) the inner voice that wants to keep you stuck, to keep you from learning and growing. It is the Saboteur who says things like, "you can't do that" and "that's rather risky" and "I'm scared." The Saboteur once served a great purpose in humanity, and in our own life. It is the Saboteur who helped the prehistoric woman at the watering hole know to check for the saber-toothed tiger. If the Saboteur were not doing her job today, you might not slam on the brakes when a child stepped in front of your car. Sometimes, however, the Saboteur gets overexcited. You may have to learn to calm the Saboteur, to curb its enthusiasm. The Saboteur actually only wants to protect you – to keep you safe from harm.

Who is your Saboteur? How do you know when your Saboteur is speaking?
How aware are you when your Saboteur sabotages you?
What is your strategy to manage your Saboteur?

MY RULES

One thing you know for certain, whether your adventure is brand new or you've been at it already for a few months or years – you know that you don't want to live by someone else's rules. You know your path is unique. You can't follow someone else's trail; it just isn't going to happen that way.

You can't pick a book off the shelf that tells you how to do this. You are designing your own trail to the top.

So, what ARE your rules? What are the rules you intend to set for yourself, to create a successful, joyful and meaningful entrepreneurial experience? Here are some questions to get you started thinking about your rules:

- What values must be honored in your work?
- How do you choose to make decisions?
- What kind of people do you want to work with as partners or as clients?
- How will you ensure your life is balanced?
- What do you want to be known for in your potential client base?
- How do you remain authentic?

MY RULES

BE AND DO STARS

To be all you want to be and to do all you want to do, you need to take stock occasionally! Who do you actually want to be and do? Complete the Be and Do Star exercise quickly and intuitively, without a lot of thought. Answer these two questions: How do I choose to Be right now? And, what am I drawn to Do? For example, a client of mine had these items on her Be list. She wants to be joyful, creative, fun to be around, purposeful, engaged. (She had more, but that may be enough to get you started!) She also found herself being drawn to Do: public speaking, quilting, volunteering, and having 100 followers on Twitter.

After you complete your stars, ask yourself, "What is the alignment between the two stars? Are the Be items attainable through the Do items? How do the Be items support the Do items? The last time I completed the stars I realized there were some very compelling Be reasons that explained my sudden fascination with watercolor. And I signed up for watercolor class! "Creative" and "learning" were in my Be star, and "watercolor" and "design" in my Do star. I saw that the "doing" of watercolor would actually help me to develop the creative side that I wanted to "be" more of.

This is a great exercise to do often, not only when starting a business adventure. Do it before vacation, on your birthday, when you return to work after New Year's, and even at the beginning of each weekend.

BE

DO

33

⛰ IMPROVISE

Or, if you like, don't do ANY of the visualizing, imagining, or dreaming on the previous pages. Instead, just show up. For a simple and inspiring read on just showing up, pick up and read *Improv Wisdom* by Patricia Ryan Madson. Just showing up means saying "yes" to whatever comes your way and following it to its natural conclusion. It means trusting your intuition and not planning a lot. It involves clarity about how a possible action lands in your belly. Does it feel right? It is a magical place of encompassing all that is in front of you and simply following your energy down any of the myriad of paths that appear. Don't tell anyone, but, truth be told, I live my own Sage Entrepreneur life somewhat aligned with the *Improv Wisdom* philosophy.

"You don't get to choose how you're going to die, or when. You can only decide how you're going to live now."
—JOAN BAEZ

⊙ Use this space to begin to imagine all the possibilities that will appear when you simply say "Yes!"

WHAT'S IN YOUR PACK #6 – EXERCISE

- Feeling stuck? Walk around the block.
- Are you discouraged? Take a hike.
- Energy down? Play ball with the dogs. Borrow the dogs if you must.
- Are the ups and downs of this adventure getting to you? Try lifting weights.
- Can't seem to hit the target with your marketing? Go shoot a few arrows from a sleek compound bow.
- Sick and tired of all this? Take a day off and go to the beach or the park.
- Feel like you have lots of competition out there? Play pickle ball or badminton.
- Juices not flowing? Plop a canoe or kayak in some water and paddle your way back to creativity.
- Head or neck hurts? Enjoy a yoga class.
- Need some direction? Hit a bucket of balls.

EXERCISE

What fun, engaging, interesting, challenging physical diversions will you employ to keep your creative juices flowing, and to keep your discouragement at bay?

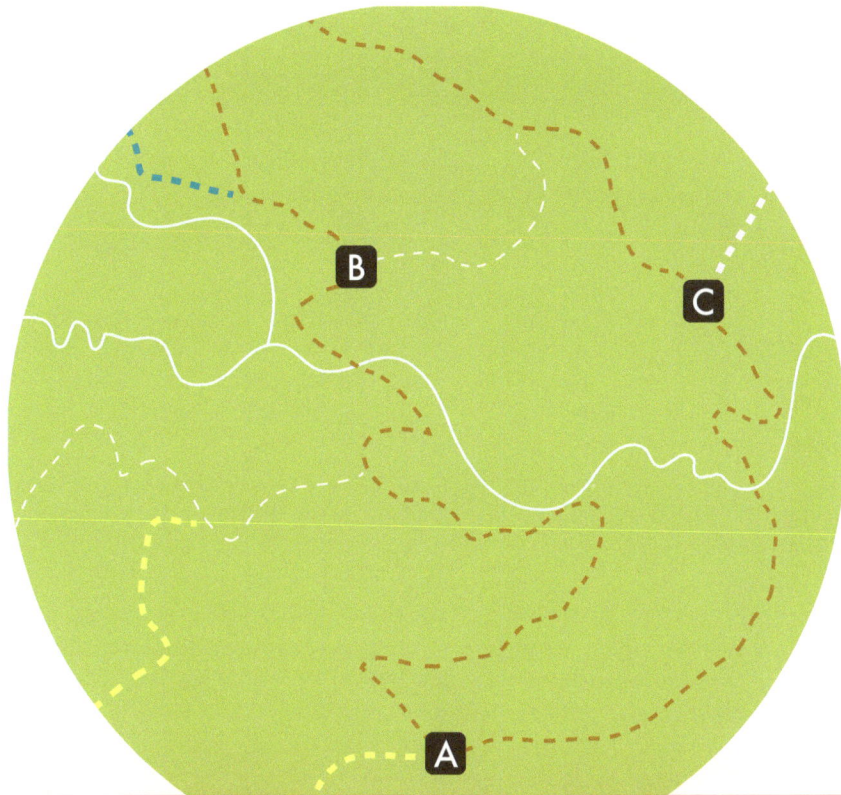

MAP
your TRAIL

MAP YOUR TRAIL

Congratulations! You have your vision; you have imagined the end of the trail. You know who you want to be and what you want to do. Your vision need not be perfect – actually, it cannot be perfect, because we are not prescient! However, your vision does need to be inspiring enough to catapult you into action. In *Map your Trail*, you will begin to act on your vision.

As you come to clearly recognize the gaps between the present state and your imagined future, questions and concerns naturally appear. You are likely asking yourself questions like these …

- What actions are the highest priorities for me to be more of who I want to be and to do more of what I want to do?
- What are the key strategies to move towards who I am becoming?
- What actions are compelling?
- What do I choose to start doing?
- What do I say no to?
- What are my beliefs, both empowering and limiting?

In this section, you will answer the most salient of these questions for your unique way of becoming a sage entrepreneur.

Right now, take a moment to commit to your vision … to do whatever you need to do for yourself to stop thinking of it as "nice to have" and to truly commit to it. You might want to do a commitment ceremony. You might want to declare it aloud to your best friend. You might want to post it for everyone (especially you!) to see. We know that there is hesitancy in thought and manifestation, until one is committed.

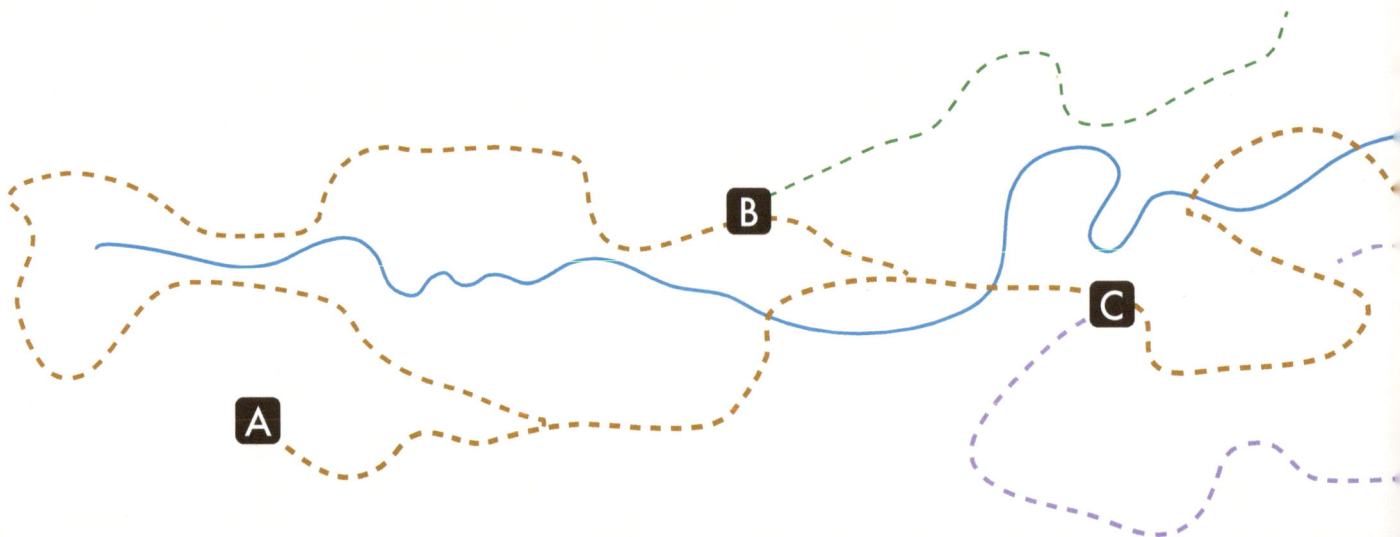

You have created a vision and your own unique rules. You've confirmed your values, strengths and life purpose. List below all the components of your work so far that you are truly committed to … all that you commit to being; all that you commit to doing.

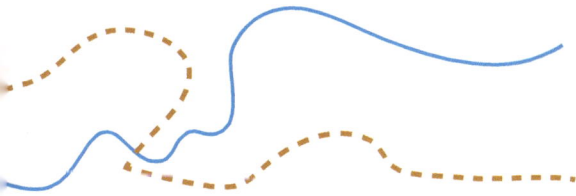

✕ WORKING BACKWARDS

There's a natural progression that will lead you to your vision. Your timeline is a bridge between today and your vision. However, there is an _unnatural_ way to map your trail. You are going to work backwards from the vision to today. There are a few reasons for this. First and foremost, there are always more tasks we can see in the short-term. This panoply of (mostly small) tasks can overwhelm the planning process. Second, it is easier to see gaps in timing and thinking when we map backwards.

The salient questions are, "What must be accomplished immediately preceding the vision? And what must be accomplished before that? And before that?"

Remember not to become bogged down by the "how" – the Backwards Map is all about the "what." Also, give yourself some time to complete this, and allow it to sit and germinate in-between versions. Be certain to include the non-work components of your Vision, as well as work ones! Here's an example of the map for this book:

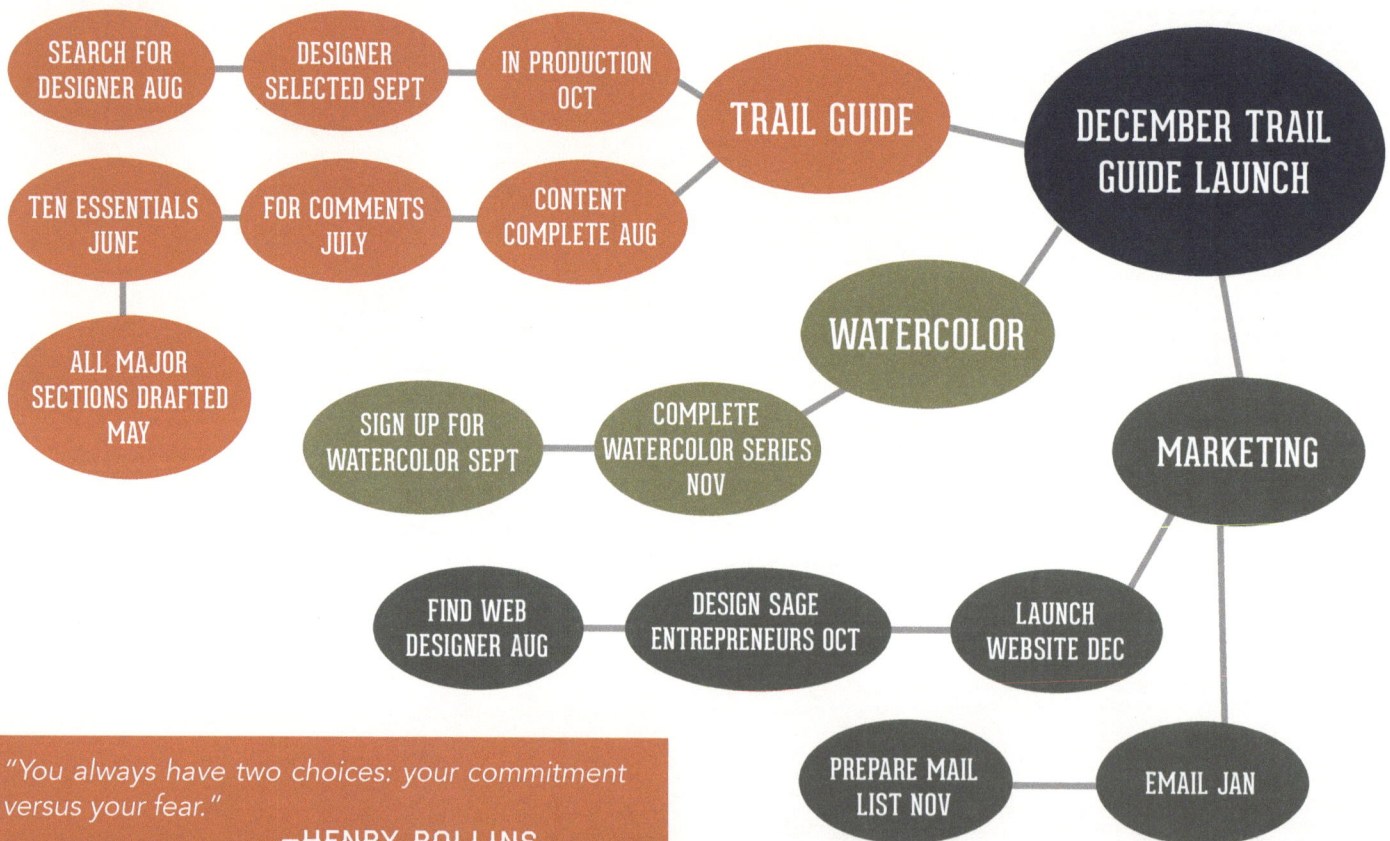

SEARCH FOR DESIGNER AUG

DESIGNER SELECTED SEPT

IN PRODUCTION OCT

TRAIL GUIDE

DECEMBER TRAIL GUIDE LAUNCH

TEN ESSENTIALS JUNE

FOR COMMENTS JULY

CONTENT COMPLETE AUG

WATERCOLOR

ALL MAJOR SECTIONS DRAFTED MAY

SIGN UP FOR WATERCOLOR SEPT

COMPLETE WATERCOLOR SERIES NOV

MARKETING

FIND WEB DESIGNER AUG

DESIGN SAGE ENTREPRENEURS OCT

LAUNCH WEBSITE DEC

PREPARE MAIL LIST NOV

EMAIL JAN

"You always have two choices: your commitment versus your fear."

—HENRY ROLLINS

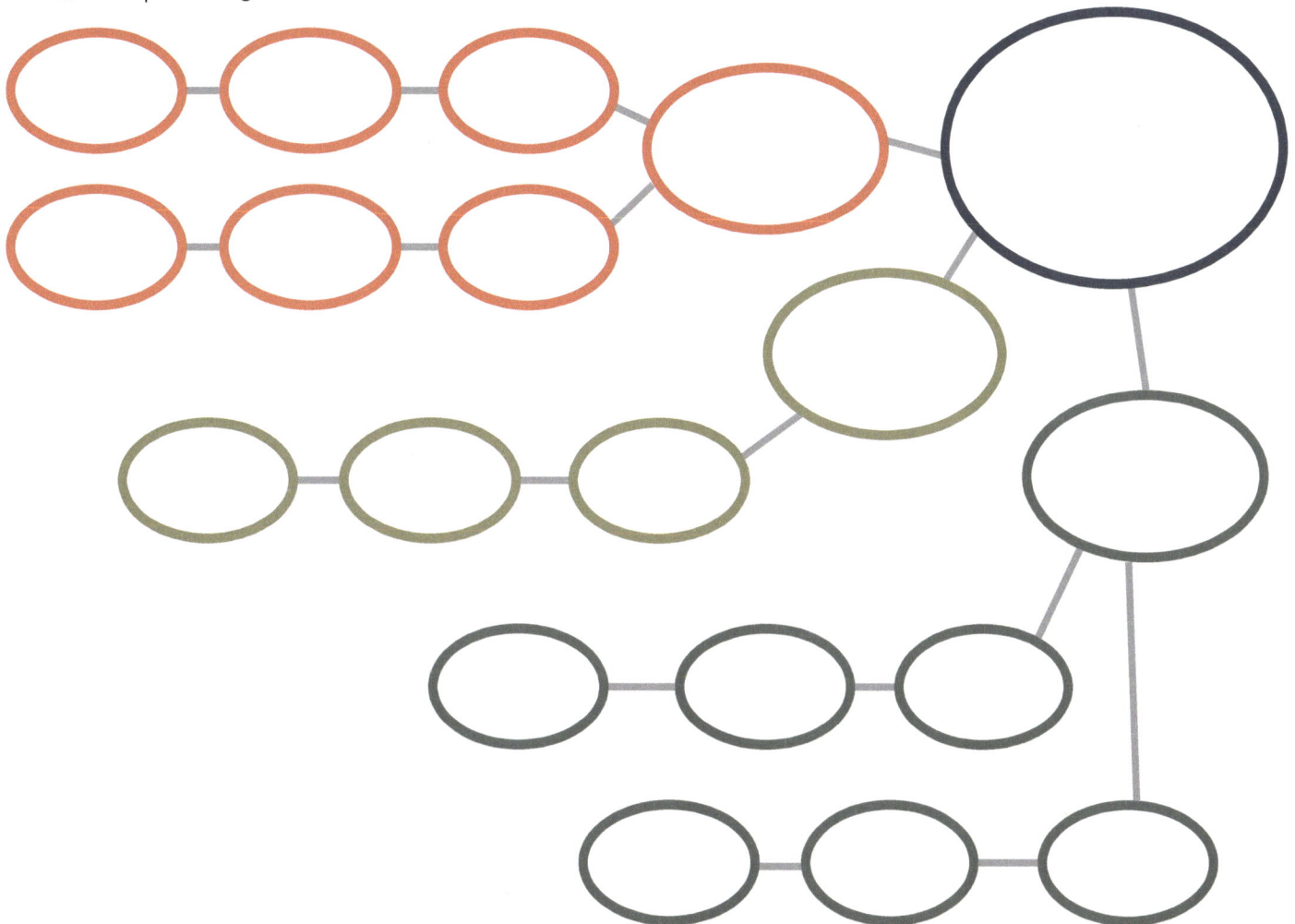

A BLANK MAP TO GET ME STARTED

Working backwards from your vision,

⊙ Put your vision in the right-hand blue circle.

⊙ What has to be accomplished right before you achieve your vision? Add three major components that must be completed right before you accomplish what's in the black circle.

⊙ And before that?

⊙ And before that?

⊙ Keep working to the left.

TRAIL JUNCTURES

As you map your trail, you will notice that you encounter small tasks to be completed, big tasks, significant goals, major milestones to reach and celebrate – all forms of Trail Junctures, where you make a decision and take action.

As you examine the map you just created, what major milestones do you see? There are probably between 3 and 10 milestones (or trail junctures – whatever terminology you like!) on your map. Identify these major trail junctures. You already have a sense of their final end date – and you may want to decide now when you intend to reach each of these trail junctures.

This next step is more traditional; it is a process you likely have used in the past. You will set actions steps to reach those milestones. This can be a very messy process! Once we transition to the specific tasks to accomplish something, our brain can easily go into overload. So have some sticky notes around, a white board, lots of paper, a piece of software you know well, whatever will help you capture random thoughts.

For example, there were many small tasks to accomplish "Launch website" in the creation of *An Entrepreneur's Trail Guide*. I had to select a website name (I bought ten of them!), draft content, decide how it would look, interview website designers, develop a spending plan, identify what reproducible handouts I wanted in the site, etc. etc. I could put all of these tasks in my visual flow chart (I did, actually). Or I could have written a list of tasks that underpin each of the major trail junctures in my flow chart. That's what I'm inviting you to do here.

Remember to set your milestones/trail junctures as well as the more specific action steps/tasks with specificity. "Make more money next year" is a very wishy-washy goal. Better is, "Earn $90,000 by December 31, 2015, a 15% increase over 2014." Be sure each goal is specific, measurable, and time-dated. Also make certain it is resonant – that is, you are excited about it!

Don't worry if you think of a task that needs to happen tomorrow and one that needs to happen 10 years from now. Just capture and write what occurs to you. And yes, you are more likely to have more tasks and more detail for action steps that are closer to today.

- ⊙ What are my major trail junctures?
- ⊙ What action steps are needed to accomplish each?

Trail Juncture/Milestone One:
Action Step/task:

①

②

③

④

⑤

Trail Juncture/Milestone Two:
Action Step/task:

①

②

③

④

⑤

If you are a typical new entrepreneur, you may find your energy was a bit drained by the last step: there's so much to do and it's overwhelming and you just want to magically reach your vision tomorrow! Congratulations if you have this reaction!

Here are a few important truths to remember about your long to-do list. First, goals can change. No, let me say that more strongly, goals WILL change. Life will happen and goals will change. Second, just because you wrote it does not mean it is set in stone! Your goals are navigational tools. If you use a GPS or a compass on the trail or in a sailboat, you know you will be moving towards a destination, but often not in a straight line. Your car GPS voice says she is "recalculating." She simply finds a different route to your destination when you go astray. Go easy on yourself. Yes, set the intention and the milestone, but don't be hard on yourself because your goal slipped. I guarantee you; your goals will slip and shift. And frankly, your vision will be better for it!

To help you smell the daises, and stop for water, a break, and perhaps a little snack along the trail, there are two more steps to take with your Trail Junctures and Action Steps list. So, get out the list, and add two columns to the right.

In the first column, indicate whether each item is S (short-term), M (medium-term) or L (long-term). You set the criteria for defining S, M & L.

Next – and here is the really important step – rate each trail juncture/milestone and each action step/task on a "Likelihood to Happen" scale of 1 to 10. Ten is "I am absolutely and completely certain this will happen" and 1 is "I don't even know why I put this on here; I am truly NOT inspired to accomplish this."

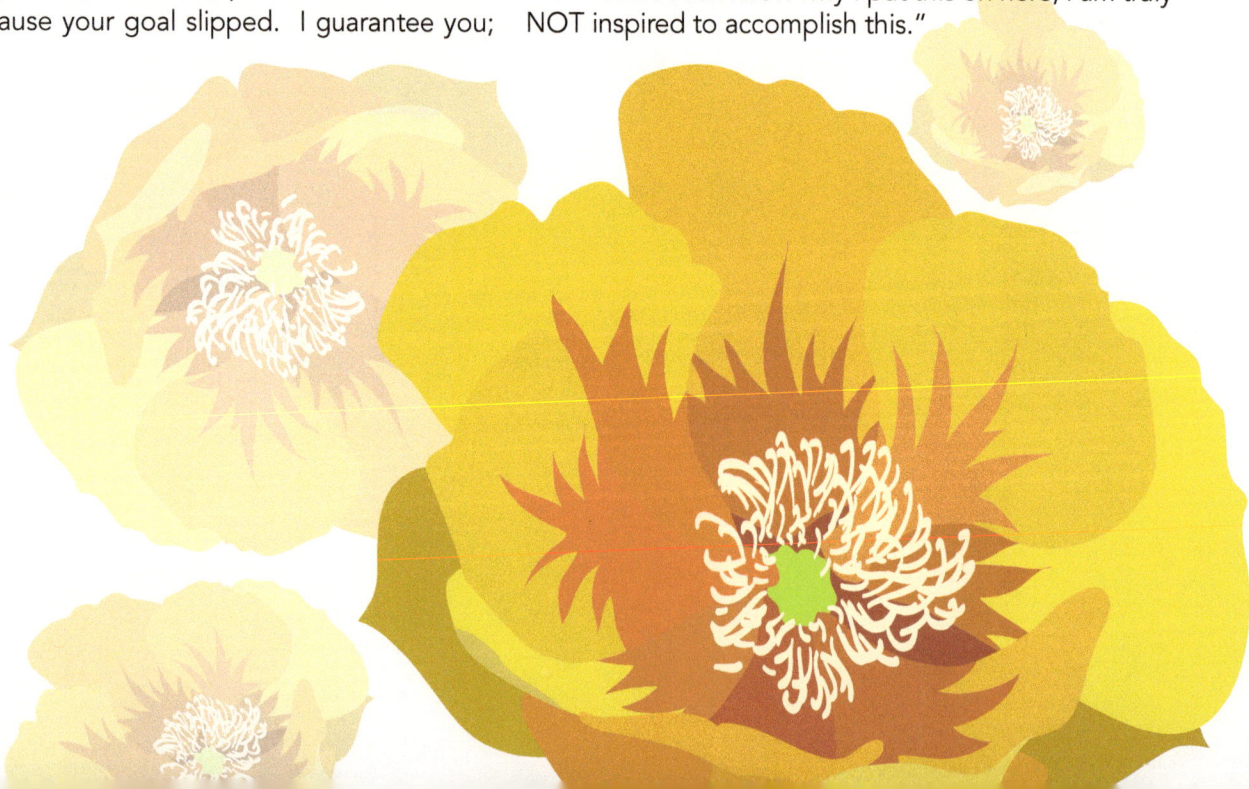

◉ On your list from the last activity, mark each item as S, M or L and rate each item on "Likelihood to happen" as a 1 to 10.

◉ OK? All done? Now, go back to every item rated 7 or lower and either: change the item, delete it, or find someone to do it. Yep, you only get to have 8's, 9's and 10's.

◉ Then, when you are done, take a long break. If you can, take a hike in the woods. Or visit a museum. Or go for a massage. Do anything that, to you, is stopping to enjoy the wildflowers.

✕ EMPOWERING BELIEFS

The moment you begin to put energy into moving forward or creating a vision, choosing a task and committing to it, Limiting Beliefs begin to appear.

Limiting Beliefs are not TRUE. They are simply beliefs. They feel true, because they can become habitual. That's all. Limiting Beliefs are stories we tell ourselves to keep ourselves from taking risks and stepping out. They are induced by fear and discomfort with the unknown. Our Limiting Beliefs want us to stay comfy and cozy, doing what we have always done and being who we have always been.

You don't have to believe your Limiting Beliefs!!! As a matter of fact, DON'T believe your Limiting Beliefs. Notice them, speak them, become clear what they are – so you can transform them (poof!) into Empowering Beliefs. What are some Limiting Beliefs you hold right now? Here's some that might be nibbling at the edges (or the center!) of your confidence:

- The economy is so bad, I'll never get work
- I don't know how to sell my service
- Maybe this business isn't viable
- Am I good enough? Compared to all of them?
- Will I ever be good at this?
- I can't find clients. At least, not enough.
- Etc., etc., etc.

Limiting Beliefs can transform into Empowering Beliefs. Beliefs drive behavior, which drive results. When you change your beliefs, you change your life.

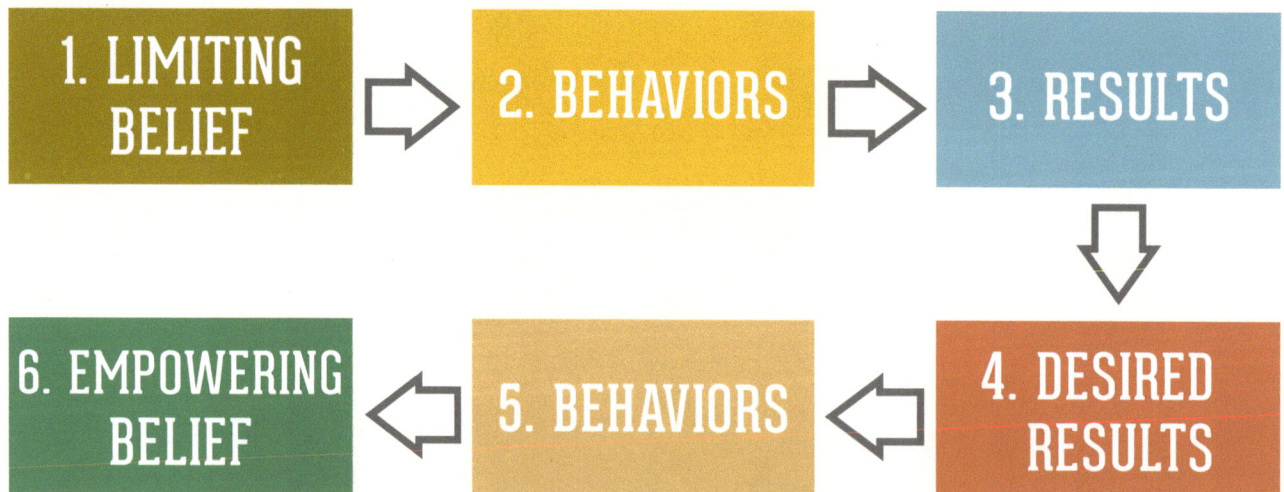

1. LIMITING BELIEF	➡	2. BEHAVIORS	➡	3. RESULTS

⬇

6. EMPOWERING BELIEF	⬅	5. BEHAVIORS	⬅	4. DESIRED RESULTS

EMPOWERING BELIEFS

A Limiting Belief I hold is: _____

Another one is _____

Now transform your Limiting Belief into an Empowering Belief. Here's a process to follow. Identify your Limiting Belief. List the behaviors you exhibit when you believe that belief ... what you do or don't do, what you say or don't say, your conduct, your physical gestures, your thoughts about yourself. After you have created an exhaustive list, identify the results you get from those behaviors. What outcomes or consequences? What action? What feelings? What fallout?

Then work backwards. Identify the results you <u>want</u>, then a list of the behaviors required to achieve those results, and finally, an Empowering Belief that you can believe as true, at least in part.

1. LIMITING BELIEF	⇨	2. BEHAVIORS	⇨	3. RESULTS
◎		◎		◎
		◎		◎
		◎		◎
		◎		◎
		◎		◎

⇩

6. EMPOWERING BELIEF	⇦	5. BEHAVIORS	⇦	4. DESIRED RESULTS
◎		◎		◎
		◎		◎
		◎		◎
		◎		◎
		◎		◎

Affirmations are the successful entrepreneur's secret weapon. Nothing works quite as well for keeping you on your journey. True, some might call this strategy "fake it till you make it." That's fine ... their tongue-in-cheek comment is absolutely correct! We affirm what we want to be true about ourselves, until it is – or until we deeply believe it.

Affirmations have rules! If you don't follow the rules, they will neither shift your internal beliefs, nor your external reality. The first rule is easy – speak and write your affirmation in the first person. It's not "Janey is a successful entrepreneur." An effective affirmation is "I am a successful entrepreneur." The second rule is your affirmation must be written in the present tense. "I will attract the perfect clients" is not an affirmation; it is an intention or a goal. An affirmation is "I attract the perfect clients" or "I am attracting the perfect clients every day." Third, and most difficult, an affirmation cannot be a negative. It simply does not set up the right energy. Instead of "I am not procrastinating" try on "I always take appropriate action in a timely manner."

That's it for rules. Now, content. You know what you need to affirm. You truly do. Here are some to get you started:
- I am confident and competent
- I speak clearly
- I excel at the service I provide
- I am joyful

Finally, what to do with your affirmations?   Do whatever it takes so you can easily remember to say (or shout!) them to yourself. Post them on your mirror, your keyboard, your pillow, your phone. Wherever you will be reminded.

My affirmations ...

Though it feels lonely at times, none of us travels our path alone. Who is there for you, supporting you, cheering you on, and providing practical or emotional support? Who do you want to add?

First, notice that your primary support team is inside of you. It may sound odd to think about your "inner" support team, but it's there! When you explored The Captain & The Saboteur, you met a very important member of your inner support team, your Captain. There are other inner support team members as well. Sometimes entrepreneurs identify people in their lives who were once inspiring and wise, such as a loving grandmother or a sage mentor. Other inner team members you might want to seek out and cultivate include the Appreciator, the Curious One, and the Creative One.

Second, there are the "outer" support team members. These are the people in your life who support you emotionally, intellectually, physically, spiritually. They may challenge you to look at situations differently, or they may be your number one cheerleader. They may remind you of your dream. They may cook dinner for you, so you can keep right on working.

INNER TEAM

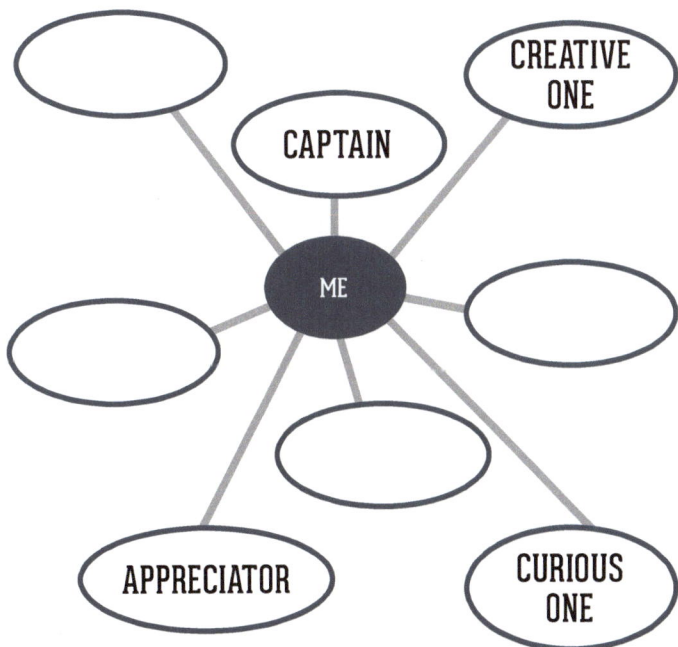

CREATIVE ONE

CAPTAIN

ME

APPRECIATOR

CURIOUS ONE

OUTER TEAM

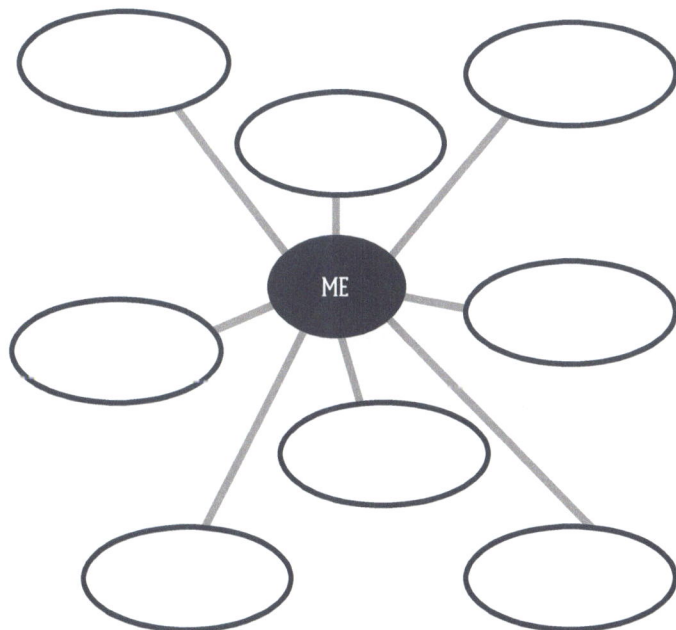

ME

SPENDING PLAN

Spending Plan – doesn't that sound way more inspiring and inviting than a "budget?" Yes, it costs money, time, energy and resources to begin your business. Fortunately, as a service entrepreneur, you don't have a lot of inventory to buy, but still there are business cards, phone lines, perhaps some software, your website to purchase and design, business licenses, maybe a service mark to research and apply for, perhaps an office to rent. You might also want a few partners ... an accountant, a coach (of course!), some administrative support.

What are your financial priorities? How much will they cost? In what order do you need to find them? Where will the funds come from?

A mistake some entrepreneurs make is to believe they must have everything all shiny and new in place before inviting in their first client. Not true! Just the other day, I was talking with an entrepreneur who owns a dog-walking business. She started walking dogs. She asked around, found a client or two among her friends and acquaintances, and then funded her spending plan from her revenues. When she had enough cash from a few dog walks, she printed off business cards and tacked them up in coffee shops and pet stores. When she had a few more dollars from a few more clients, she built a website. She built her business directly from the revenues she generated. In the days of Facebook and LinkedIn, there are many direct routes to prospects.

- ⊙ What are my priorities?
- ⊙ How much will each priority cost?
- ⊙ Where will the funds come from?
- ⊙ What's coming in?
- ⊙ What's going out?

WHAT'S COMING IN

DESCRIPTION	AMOUNT
1	
2	
3	
4	
5	
6	
7	
8	
9	
10	

WHAT'S GOING OUT
FIXED

DESCRIPTION	AMOUNT
1	
2	
3	
4	
5	
6	
7	
8	
9	
10	

WHAT'S GOING OUT
VARIABLE

DESCRIPTION	AMOUNT
1	
2	
3	
4	
5	
6	
7	
8	
9	
10	

Invitation
By Ann Betz in "Coaching the Spirit"

There is a door I want to pass through
and you've offered
to hold it open so I can stand
and look at a distant land

It's bright there and fun and terrifying
and as you gaze at me with steady eyes
you never stop saying
"I see you here"

And this statement of belonging
which you speak so matter-of-factly
buoys me, calms my heart
and carries me over
the threshold to where I want to be

My Invitation to Myself is...

BOOTS

ON!

BOOTS ON!

In this step, you implement the strategies. Step by step, your boots supporting and protecting your feet, you travel towards your destination. Together we assess what is working, and what needs to change. Together we build accountability. Together we celebrate successes.

"There comes a time when what is needed is not just rhetoric, but boots on the ground."

—BALDWIN SPENCER

CAIRNS

On many hiking trails, especially in the desert, cairns mark the way. Typically they don't indicate an exact path, but they do spot a general direction. If you ever hike in red rock country, you may see these rock signposts. Now that you have completed your vision and mapped your trail, certain cairns will mark your path. Since you are writing your own rules, you will also be making your own cairns.

To keep you true to these cairns, to keep you somewhat on the path you intend to follow, you may find it quite useful to have some accountability partners. Your coach can be an excellent accountability partner, and so can others in your life. Perhaps you will join a small group of other entrepreneurs, who make commitments to one another, and support each other in completing those commitments. Perhaps your mom or your best friend can be a great accountability partner to you. Your accountability to yourself is also, of course, foremost.

For example, a key cairn of a client of mine was "To launch a product by the end of 2014." Another one of his cairns was "To begin a contract with a XX company or YY company by July 31, 2015." For his product cairn, he joined with a small group of entrepreneurs who held him accountable, as well as provided ideas, suggestions, laughter, wine, and support. For his cairn on establishing a contract with a new company, he worked with his coach to set up accountability.

Choose some key cairns and design an accountability that feels supportive, exciting, and doable.

- What are your cairns?

- And who will help hold you to your accountabilities?

"My optimism wears heavy boots and is loud"
—HENRY ROLLINS

WHAT'S IN YOUR PACK? – MINDFULNESS

Amidst the tumult and turmoil of being a sage entrepreneur, there are few natural places to stop and rest. The stress and anxiety, as well as the joy and excitement, can keep you on a roller coaster and ultimately sap your energy. Mindfulness is how we overcome this stress. Mindfulness is a state of being present and aware. There are many ways to be mindful. We can increase our mindfulness in eating, taking a shower or doing the dishes, or stopping to mindfully take a walk, pray or meditate. Being in the wilderness can be a mindful experience; journaling is useful for some.

Even just five minutes away of quiet, intentional meditation can keep you grounded. Meditation is proven to reinforce our health, from lowering blood pressure and stress, to increasing your sense of well-being.

To begin to meditate is not hard. A few suggestions:
- Sit up straight and close your eyes.
- Focus on your breath. Notice it flowing in through your nostrils, filling your belly, and going out again. Notice how it changes the shape of your back. If you are able, feel it flowing through your body.
- When thoughts come in, and your mind begins to plan, decide, remember, solve ... simply return to your breath.

Do not judge yourself when you notice that thoughts have taken over. Simply return to a focus on the breath.

Many people who meditate find moving meditation to be beneficial. This is a finger labyrinth – a meditation tool. Very slowly and intentionally, move your finger along the path, while focusing on your breath. Travel in to the center, and then retrace your path back to the starting point.

COMPLETE THE FINGER LABYRINTH

BEGIN HERE

61

FEEDBACK LOOP

As an entrepreneur, you will experience feedback ALL the time. You send out a blog, and someone makes a positive comment. You hand your business card to another professional who says "Cool card!" You place an ad in your local paper and receive no – count 'em – zero responses. You deliver your service and your client says, "It was great, but …"

Feedback is the entrepreneur's muse. It is a golden tablet. Would that you receive feedback instead of apathy! There is no reason to judge it (or yourself!) as good or bad, it simply is. You make a decision, take an action, and some result occurs. That's simply the way of the world. The only way to eliminate all "bad" feedback is to take no action.

AND, the only way to make meaning of the feedback loop is to learn. You might decide to pivot; to make a change and do something different. You might simply notice the results and do nothing different. You might ramp up your efforts.

Keep learning! Every action you take is an opportunity to learn.

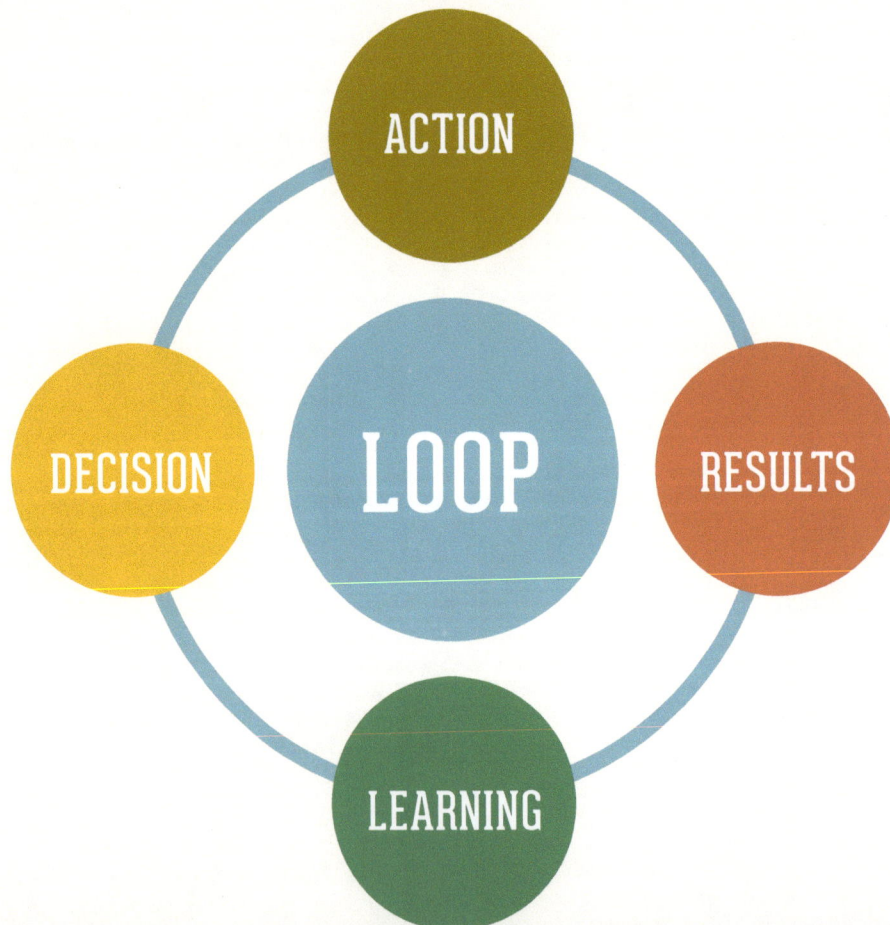

ACTION

RESULTS

LOOP

LEARNING

DECISION

WHAT FEEDBACK HAVE I RECEIVED?

◉ An action I took:

The results:

What I learned:

What I decided:

◉ Another action I took:

The results:

What I learned:

What I decided:

◉ An action I intend to take:

What I hope the results will be:

What I can learn:

What decision will this inform?

(This excellent exercise has been borrowed from Joe Abraham's insightful book, *Entrepreneurial DNA*.)

This may feel like a visioning exercise, however, I give it to you now because I believe it is most effective when you have some action under your belt; when you've tried some strategies and they have been wildly successful, and you have initiated others that fell flat on their behinds. It is also a great exercise to conduct before embarking on any project, large or small.

The A, B, C Scenarios exercise allows you to create three very different scenarios, so you can decide what is right for you at this time.

Scenario A is the worst case, minimum scenario. It requires the least effort and will generate the lowest results. For example, my Scenario A for *An Entrepreneur's Trail Guide* was complete my book, sell a few, gain a few clients, and stroll into retirement.

Scenario B is the realistic, average scenario. You invest more time and energy; you anticipate higher results. My Scenario B: implement social media, find other entrepreneurs to market to, fill my practice, and sell a hundred books every year through a distributor.

Scenario C is the best case, "swing for the fence" scenario. You spare no expense and no effort. You go for it, completely. Scenario C for *An Entrepreneur's Trail Guide*: Fill my practice with entrepreneurs, take on two or more protégés, sell thousands of books, and hire someone to do all the marketing.

Abraham tells us it is very important to look at all three scenarios, even though two of them likely don't excite you very much. It allows you to choose a scenario that stretches you, while accommodating your current capacity.

Scenario A:

Scenario B:

Scenario C:

◉ Which scenario captures your interest?

◉ Which do you have the capacity for (financial, knowledge, energy, resources...)?

◉ Which is a stretch for you?

◉ What components do you want to shift (you can steal one from C and add it to A, if you want!) into your final scenario?

◉ What's next?

GROWING

With boots on your feet, your journey is underway. There will constantly be new vistas to see, unexpected turns in the trail, rocks to stumble over, and inclement weather to deal with. As you travel this path, you must keep growing. Sure, you may decide to grow your client base. Yes, you may decide to expand your services. Perhaps you'll choose to hire some employees or sub-contractors. How fast and how big you grow is up to you.

What I most want to address now is your own growth. Starting your own entrepreneurial ventures forces you into self-development. It causes you to pause and examine – how confident am I? How competent? It exposes you to all kinds of emotions you may not otherwise feel – fear, shame uncertainty, elation, joy, astonishment, perplexity. It pushes you to acknowledge that you don't understand accounting and you never did get around to setting up a blog. It invites you to learn more about so many realms you never knew anything about – budgeting, negotiations, marketing, selling, publicity, social media, as well as all it takes to keep current in you professional expertise. It is not for the meek of heart. It takes courage, commitment, and above all, resiliency.

You MUST keep learning and growing, just to keep your business stable.

- How will I keep growing?

- What specific classes will I take?

- What books will I read?

- Who will I stay connected to, to keep me vital?

- How will I stay current, and even ahead of the game?

- Who inside my field do I need to learn from?

- Who outside my field can help me expand my perspective, my view of the world, and my knowledge?

- Who can I mentor or teach?

RELISH
the VIEW

RELISH THE VIEW

Now you have arrived at the top. At the place of Be-ing. When you Relish the View you are participating in the dance of life. As we approach a pure sense of being who we want to be, we tweak, we flex, we adjust, we reposition, we re-imagine. It is juicy and engaging to be immersed in such a process, consciously engaged and powerfully present.

Here, you are able to Be all you want to be, and to Do all you want to do.

"I exist as I am, that is enough."
–WALT WHITMAN

Celebrating? It's not something we are very good at in our culture. Oh yes, we celebrate birthdays, anniversaries, and promotions. But stopping to celebrate the small wins, especially the wins that come about as a result of our hard work, or our good luck, or our special insight, or our amazing intuition ... these we celebrate poorly.

Especially early in our entrepreneurial journey, when clients are few and far between, and when most of our efforts are on networking, and mapping our trail, and envisioning our future, it is really important to celebrate our successes, our good luck, and even our failures. Rituals to reinforce our self-confidence and our efforts help to keep us positive, upbeat, and inspired.

Celebrations can be big or small, expensive or cost nothing at all. What's important is to pause, reflect, and pat ourselves on the back. You can celebrate by having a coffee on the deck on a warm summer day. You can take the dog out for an extra walk. You can treat yourself to a juicy peach or a bowl of mint chocolate chip ice cream. You can buy that bottle of wine you've been eyeballing. You can get a massage (or give one!) The best celebrations include other people, especially those on your support team. Call your best friend and tell him you met three potential clients at a networking meeting. Take one of your kids with you for that peach ice cream and tell them you are proud of yourself.

CELEBRATION
What can you celebrate right now, today, at this stage of your journey?
List at least ten items.

Now, how will you celebrate? And when? How about right this very minute?

Entrepreneurial DNA by Joe Abraham. Not all entrepreneurs are the same! Serial entrepreneurs don't manage their ventures anything like expert entrepreneurs. Take the instrument and you'll learn about what type entrepreneur you are. Plus, you'll stop comparing yourself with entrepreneurs who seem to thrive differently.

How to Train a Wild Elephant by Jan Chozen Bays. Lots of books on mindfulness are so serious! I like this one especially, with fifty mindfulness exercises. You can read and try on one a week for almost an entire year.

Coaching the Spirit by Ann Betz & Jacek Skrzypczynski. This small book is an inspiration to coaches and their clients alike.

The Inspired Business Approach by Leslie Lupinsky and Joni Mar. This practical and enjoyable book will help you with enrolling clients, niches, and marketing – especially for service professionals. Available at www.leslielupinskyintl.com.

Improv Wisdom by Patricia Ryan Madson. This book presents 13 maxims of improvisation theater, applied to real life. Maxims like "say yes" and "just show up" offer powerful wisdom for entrepreneurs and all life-livers.

StrengthsFinder 2.0 by Tom Rath. Use the one-time-only code in the back of the book to complete the StrengthsFinder instrument online and receive a report on your top five strengths. Then read about your strengths and the strengths of people who matter to you.

Is Your Genius at Work? by Dick Richards. You can spend lots of money uncovering your unique genius – or you can buy Mr. Richards book and find it on your own. The exercises in this book are fun and enlightening.

Website Resources. For more resources and additional workbook pages from *An Entrepreneur's Trail Guide*, please visit SageCoach.com/SageEntrepreneur

An Entrepreneur's Trail Guide provides a fun and effective way to uncover your dreams, values, and strengths — all that you need to create a new path that will make you happy and successful. Andrea Sigetich has put tremendous wisdom on these pages for readers to easily access. She has given all of her readers a wonderful gift.
Prof. Kathy E. Kram, Shipley Professor in Management, Boston University

Andrea has been my "Sage" for more than 15 years. Working with her will guide you in making the most effective choices in your entrepreneurial adventure.
Donna Billings, Author, Coach & World Traveler

It has been said that one should not seek what is lacking in the world and try to fill that gap; but, rather to seek to know your gift and take that to the world. As my coach, Andrea has brought me through the forest and into the open trail of my gifts, with power. This book is a clear "How To" guide of that process.
Dennis Doherty, Entrepreneur and Coach

Andrea has a keen ability for getting at the heart of an issue in a clear, no nonsense, and compassionate way.
Hendy Dayton, Executive Coach

I read anything Andrea writes because she is wise, enthusiastic, optimistic, and committed to making things work.
Carolyn Esky, Adjunct Professor, Human Development, Central Oregon Community College

ABOUT ANDREA

With the demeanor of a sage, leavened with a strong dose of animation, Andrea brings years of leadership experience to her work as a coach. Before opening SageCoach in 1997, and leading a highly successful entrepreneurial adventure ever since, Andrea held senior leadership positions in Fortune 500 technology organizations. Her extensive client list includes both large and small organizations, from FedEx to Deschutes Brewery to entrepreneur coaches, accountants, and other professionals. She also is a faculty member for the Coaches Training Institute (CTI).

Andrea enthusiastically pursues desert hiking (obviously!) as well as kayaking and improv theater from her home in Bend, Oregon which she shares with her husband, Beryl Rullman, three cats, and two delightfully active Springer Spaniels. Andrea wrote and published (by Career Press) a book with her colleague Carol Leavitt, *Play to Your Strengths*.